## Authors Word:

I opted not to have a big name foreword and instead choose to share with you why I wrote this book. I have been publishing books for the last 5 years and discovered a simple system that anyone can use to not only publish but also promote to a Best Seller Status.

I have found that the 10 Billion dollar e-book industry has spawned a plethora of publishers that are charging egregious rates. I am on a mission to produce good books at fair prices. The information contained herein will allow an average author to self publish effectively and earn income and gain market share.

*Johnny "MACKnificent" Mack*

Self Publish Your Own Book

# Copyright Page

Copyright ⓒ 2015 by Johnny "MACKnificent" Mack
All rights reserved, No part of this publication may be reproduced, distributed, or transmitted in any form or by any means, including photocopying, recording, or other mechanical methods, without the prior written permission of the publisher, except in the case of brief quotations embodied in critical reviews and certain other noncommercial uses permitted by copyright law. For permission requests, write to the publisher, addressed "Attention: Permissions Coordinator," at the address below.
Self Published Authors Network
Ordering information
Quantity Sales. Special discounts are available in quantity purchases by corporations, associations, networking groups. For details contact www.SelfPublishedAuthorsNetwork the address above
Individual Sales- Contact Johnny "MACKnificent" Mack @469-537-8905
www.selfpublishingnetwork.com
Includes biographical references and index

## Acknowledgements

Dr. John freeman

Rev. Rene Chandler

Angela Butler

John McClung Jr.

Terrance Leftridge

Edward C. Williams

Keylend Wright

Carl Randolph

Gwen Cunningham-Jones

Gerald P. Simmons

Dr. Edward Womack

Dr. Ruben West

## Dedication Page

This book is Dedicated to Everybody that has a book in them. I have found that EVERYBODY has a book in them. Everybody has something that they need to say and that they want to say. Everyone I run into wants to tell their story or tell a story and feel that they have a story to tell. this book is about HOW to tell that story and HOW to use the best practices to make sure that the story not only gets told but also it gets told in a manner that leads to it being a best seller.

Most people feel that their story is unique and special. I believe it is and that it needs to be told. Before now the possibility of getting your story told or in print required luck or lots of money. Technology has transformed the arena and made the marketplace equal for everyone.

this book exposes that equality and shows you how to become a published AND bestselling author.

This book is also dedicated to the first ten people I have helped to get their books published and launched into best seller status.

# Self Publish Your Own Book

## Contents

| | |
|---|---|
| Authors Word: | 1 |
| Copyright Page | 2 |
| Acknowledgements | 3 |
| Dedication Page | 4 |
| Introduction | 8 |
| Step 1~Title | 26 |
| Step2~Outline | 33 |
| Step3~Unload your Mind | 40 |
| Step5~ Mind Map | 44 |
| Step 6~Clump It | 48 |
| Step7~ Content | 56 |
| Step 8~ Proof & Edit | 64 |
| Step 9~ Final Proof Yourself | 74 |
| Step10~CreateSpace | 76 |
| Step 11~ Kindle | 94 |
| Step 12~ ABS (Automatic Best Seller) | 100 |
| Prologue: | 104 |

# Self Publish Your Own Book

## Introduction

You have to answer 5 questions before you publish your Book:

- What do you want to write about
- Why do you want to write about that
- When do you want to write it
- Where do you want to publish it (Print or e-book)
- Who will help you publish and promote it

# Self Publish Your Own Book

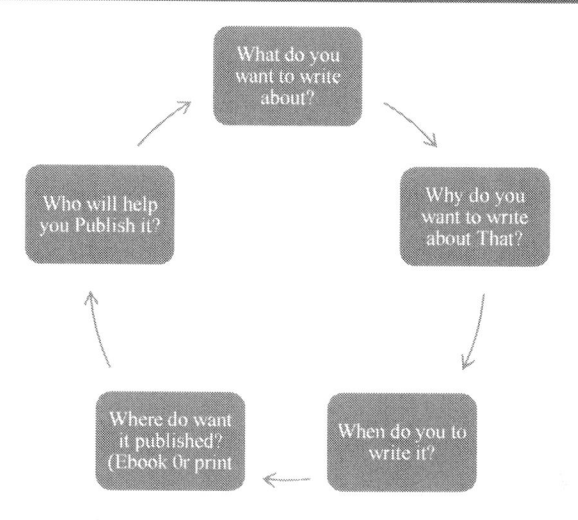

- What do you want to write about?
- Why do you want to write about That?
- When do you to write it?
- Where do want it published? (Ebook Or print)
- Who will help you Publish it?

Surprisingly the answer to these five crucial questions will determine if you are ready to publish a book or if you are just thinking about it. When you are serious about writing and publishing a book you are able to deal with anything and the little things that distract and derail the average person will not hinder you.

What you choose as a topic is very important. The title is a offshoot of what you are writing about. Most people choose a catchy title and try and write around it.

Whether you pick a title first or last, the WHAT factor is still of paramount importance. You see your What will determine everything from your audience to your genre.

There cannot be enough said about what you plan to write about. When you have effectively answered this question then the others become easier to answer. Your **What** is the reason you are writing in the first place. You can look back over all your life and see that once **WHAT** has been answered the **How** and all other matters become crystal clear. That Clarity is the essence of accomplishment.

Stop wasting your time on How you are going to accomplish the task and begin asking what it is you want to do. With the book, as in life, your WHAT is the starting point. The key to any type of success is to get started.

Most people never succeed because they never get going.  A multitude of error can be corrected just by beginning, "**it is in not trying that most men fail**".  The **What** is the beginning that is necessary to get your book done.

Take some time to decide What your Title will be and What you are writing about.  There are several What's that have to be answered.

- What is the topic you want to write on
- What is the Title going to be
- What is the length of the book you plan on writing
- What is the genre you plan to write in
- What do you hope to accomplish by writing a book
- What will you do once it is written

- What are you willing to give up in order to complete the book
- What are you willing to invest in order to get your book published
- What steps have you taken to get a book completed and published
- What is the next step you plan to take to get published

Once you have complete Clarity on What it is you want to accomplish regarding your book, the next question is Why. In answering what, you will have already answered half the question.

When you determine your **What** your **Why** just becomes a definition. You need to know **Why** or the **What** gets lost in translation. Your **Why** is the fuel to get the What going. Unless you have a clear answer as to **Why** you want to write a book, it will languish on the I'm gonna stage for years.

I have coached authors that have had completed manuscripts gathering dust for years because their **Why** was unanswered. The **Why** is what will wake you up to write and not let you go to sleep at night. Your **Why** is the passion and the purpose.

With a clarity on their **Why** those authors would have published books and be enjoying the benefits of having done so. Because they wrote a book without being clear as to **Why** they found themselves in a murky place. They were unable to find the necessary skill set to finish in that they did not know why they wanted to in the first place.

The **Why** answers a very important question...**WHY**. **Why** are you willing to subject yourself to the grind and the gripping dread of writing a book. **Why** would you put yourself though the pain and the agony of writing and rewriting and being rejected. Only a person that is Clear about What they want to say and **Why** they want to say is willing to endure that torture. The question of Why is broken down into several key components...

- Why do you want to write a book
- Why do you feel you are capable of writing a book
- Why do you feel you are competent to write a book

- Why do you feel anyone wants to read what you have to say
- Why do you feel writing a book meets any unanswered questions
- Why Now and not later
- Why is that topic relevant
- Why do you feel you are able to write about that topic
- Why Do you feel people will read what you have to say on that topic
- Why is this What important to you

Once you have these two cornerstone questions answered everything else is just gravy. But there are still a few questions that have to be answered. It's important to know **When** you want to publish your book. This answers a very crucial question and sets up a timeline that can be defended.

Once you have a date and time established you will find time and opportunity to complete the project. A dream without a deadline is just a wish. If wishes were cars we'd all be driving.

The question of **When** points the author toward a timetable and deadline. If you have a projected date as to **When** you plan on being finished, you will schedule time and focus with renewed anticipation.

Until you have a specific date and time, you just have a nebulous future event...One day I'm going to write a book. With a timeframe of When that **'Someday'** becomes one day with a framework on it.

Knowing **When** prompts you to begin and to keep on a timeline. A timeline is the key to completing your book. If you are operating without an endpoint, you can become easily distracted and find that there is no needed discipline in place. **WHEN** is a litmus test that positions the writer in specific timeframe that allows and demands that you stay on track.

It is so easy to put your book and writing it on the back burner. There is never enough time or the time you have you can get so busy in that you are never able to get around to writing. If you have a dedicated timeframe, it becomes not only easy but also necessary to have a regular writing regimen and time slot.

When the question of **WHEN** is answered the other answers are easily put into place and the finished product comes into being. There are 10 key factors regarding When...

- When do you want to Publish it
- When are you going to schedule time to write it
- When do you plan on publishing it
- When are you going to release it
- When do you want to be finished researching it
- When will you get it edited and Proofed
- When do you want it available for public viewing
- When are you going to start on it
- When will you begin promoting it
- When will you stop procrastinating

What and Why without When only amounts to a frustrated future.

Another key question and component is that of **Where**. Whereas What, Why and When are of utmost importance, **WHERE** is on the same level. This begs to answer the question of Where. **Where** do you want to publish it at. As a Kindle or as an e-book or as a print paperback. Do you only want it available online or do you want to have a product in hand to verify and validate. Are you interested in having the book available in bookstores.

The location or **Where** is extremely importance. Knowing and having Clarity as to the location of Where you want your book to be available is sensible and salient. It is sensible because it gives you an understanding of the direction you want your book to go. It is salient because it gives you an out of the box criteria of exactly **Where** you can begin pre-marketing and get your best ROI. There are several questions regarding **Where** that must be answered...

- Where do you want to have book published
- Where don't you want to offer the book
- Where do you want to promote your book
- Where do you want to distribute your Book
- Where do you want to host your Book Signings
- Where do you want your book available (online-stores)
- Where do you want to see your book displayed

- Where do you want your book to grow to

No question Those four questions are the cornerstone of building your new Self Published book. There is yet one question that must be answered and that is Who.

Who is going to be able and willing to help you get your book published. Who is a question that fills in the gap. It allows you to engage in collaboration with others to complete your project.

There are many people willing to assist you, you just have to ask. People want to help you they are just too afraid that they will be dismissed or laughed at. The question of Who is one that must be answered.

You can only do so much alone. There are at least ten questions that must be answered regarding Who...

- Who is able to help you edit the book
- Who is able to help you proof the book
- Who is able to help promote the book
- Who would be willing to purchase the book
- Who would be willing to give you a review
- Who would be willing to share the book on social Media
- Who is in your social media that you could market to
- Who would be willing to pre-order the book
- Who would host a book party for you

- Who would attend a book signing for your book

Once all five of these questions are answered you are ready to begin the process of Self Publishing Your Own Book and Making It A Best Seller.

# Self Publish Your Own Book

## Step 1~Title

Step 1: Select Title

Selecting a title is perhaps as important a task as any. To seriously and successful complete this task it requires more forethought than just writing down a clever title. Your title sets the tone for the entire project. You need to research it and make sure it resonates with you as well as a potential audience.

Just picking a title, any title, can cause you more work in the long run. The final title of your book has to be congruent with the point and the statement you are trying to make. If you are going to be talking about Fishing and your title is about climbing a mountain, you have failed your audience.

They will pick up the book thinking it has to do with mountain climbing or at best overcoming a huge obstacle and surprised or even disappointed that it really is about Fish.

Your title is the invitation to come in and discover what you have to say. if you have a seafood restaurant and advertise steak and chicken, you will miss out on most of your interested clientele. Also you will cause the ones that came in to be angry that you got them there under false pretenses. Take your time and be deliberate about the title of your book.

Do some Keyword research and also some interest research. Make sure your title is able to reach your intended audience. Google your purposed title and make sure it has not already been published. If it has been used before, you will find yourself in competition with another book.

This will cause confusion and likely siphon off potential sales from your book. The big downside is if the other book is poor quality or negative in a sense it will cast a pallor on your work. Do not create an obstacle for yourself before you begin. Take the extra time to get the title right

There are many tools on line that can help you get a terrific title. Just know what you want to say first and the title should somehow morph into being. I will talk about content creation and outlining in other sections of this book.

The cool thing about the outline is once you have Clarity as to what you are planning to say in your book, the title will become more obvious. You do not have to have a title to wrap the book around. Sometimes you can create a book and wrap the title around it.

Please do not take lightly the importance of the title. It is as important or more important than the cover and or the content. In the process of selling and marketing your book a proper and powerful title will take your book further than a weak or poor selected one will.

It only takes a little extra time to come up with a title that not only speaks to the purpose of the book, but also grabs the attention of the intended audience.

Do not be afraid to change your title several times during the creation of your book. Nothing is written in stone until the printer has printed the book. In the manuscript stage remember you have complete liberty and control over the finished work.

In this new age of POD (Print On Demand) technology you can change your book in an instant. If it does not resonate with the audience or if you get an inspiration , you can change it to suit or fit your mood.

Begin your title selection immediate. Write down five to ten titles you feel will convey your sentiments. It would be a good idea to have friends vote on what they think sounds good. you may even do a social media contest to help you pick the best title.

Remember you are writing to an audience. What it says to you is not as important as to what it says to your intended audience. You may want to say or convey a specific idea, yet you may need to present it in such a way that THEY get it. Your primary task is to your buying public. If they don't Get it then what was the point.

So let's recap: the Title is~

- Important
- must Resonate with your intended audience
- Can Be Changed over time
- Should be researched
- Should cause an impact
- Should indicate what the book is about
- Should be able to stick in the readers mind
- Should not be so clever it misses it's point
- Is as important as the Content or Cover

Research your Title + Review your Ritle = Choose your Title

## Step2~Outline

Next in line is the Outline. Outlining your book is crucial. It allows you to put a plan into motion as to exactly what you want to say. Your book Outline will give you a roadmap to exactly where you want to go.

Creating an outline allows you to finally get the idea out of your head and onto paper. A proper outline will give you the tool needed to complete the book in record time.

The reason most people never complete a book is they have ideas scattered all throughout their mind. They are unable to get hold of a specific direction to begin with.

They jump from idea to idea with no end in sight. they have so much to say they generally get over whelmed. They look at the task ahead and it looks so daunting that they tend to quit or postpone the process.

A simple outline holds the writer accountable and gives complete Clarity to the subject matter. It is like wanting to go somewhere and the travel agent asks "where do you want to go"? You answer "I don't know, I just want to get away from Here"

If you end up in China but you really want to go to Brazil, you have a problem. To enter the task of writing a book with no clear direction or roadmap is frustration at best and ludicrous at worse. You will flounder about and never seem to get a clear focus on what you are doing.

With a well thought out outline , you can pick up the project at anytime and be back on track. This is what will allow you to write it in a weekend. Having that outline gives you leeway to put the finishing flesh on those bones and have a finished project in little to no time.

So how do you complete Or prepare the outline itself. I'm Glad you asked. It is simpler than you might think. You see you have the idea for a book in your mind. You think this could be a Best seller if I could only get it written. If you sit down and think of everything you want to say and start jotting those ideas down, soon you will have the rudiment for an outline.

I will discuss in another section about the importance of a Brain Dump, where you write down every possible aspect that you might include in the book.

The outline is just a section by section structure of what you plan on presenting in the book. In other words the Key elements you want to discuss and the key aspects you want the reader to take away.

It should include all the chapters you want to write about and maybe some subchapters. An outline will position you to be able to speak your book in a later exercise in order to get it completed quicker. I will discuss that technique in a later section of the book.

To recap: An Outline~

- Is a recap of what the book will be
- Organizes you to write the book
- Gives focus to the project
- Stop Frustration and Overwhelm
- Gives you a roadmap to follow
- Eliminates potential timewasters
- Structures you to be able to complete the project

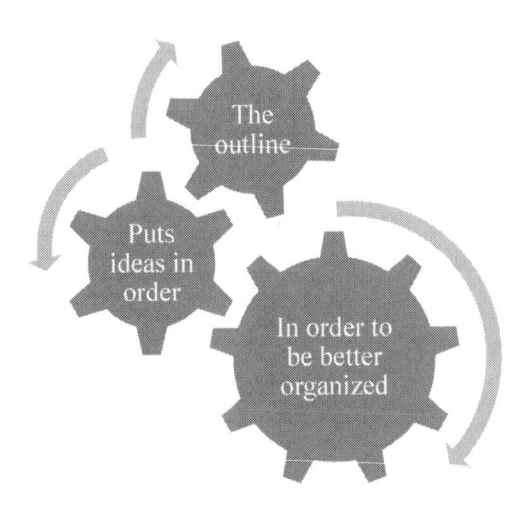

The outline

Puts ideas in order

In order to be better organized

## Step3~Unload your Mind

This section is huge, it deals with doing a data dump of your mind. In essence it is about taking the outline and sitting down to think of every possible thing you can about this potential book.

You just write it down and don't worry about whether you are going to use it or not. The idea is to consider every possible idea that pops in your head. You dump it all out. Some of it you will use some you won't.

This dumping is a way of ridding your mind of all the Head thrash that is surrounding the book. You usually have tons of things you could say or would say. Once you rid your head of all the possible things you have a clear mind and then you get to sort out what works for this book and what doesn't.

The Data dump is a prelude to the Mind Map. With the data Dump you are just removing all the possibilities from your head. They are triggered by the outline.

There is a natural progression. First the Title triggered all sorts of ideas which lead to the outline. The outline triggered even more thoughts which lead to the Unload.

The Process of unloading all that Stuff frees you up to be able now to actually write what you feel you want to say. Sometimes it's good just to see some of the things that were clogging your creativity. You may look at them and realize you DON'T want to include that.

In any event you now have a emptied mind and a full sheet of what you can, what you should and what you might write about. Don't feel compelled to include anything from this exercise. Or you may feel lead to include it all.

Here is a recap of this section: Unload your Mind to ~

✓ Sort out all possible content
✓ Discover potential input
✓ Unclog your mind to begin writing
✓ Consider what you MIGHT write
✓ Determine what you will not write

✓ Remove clutter from the mind

## Unload
## Head
## Trash

## Step5~ Mind Map

This of course leads to the incredible Mind Map. When you have completed the data dump or the mind unwind or unload, you need to begin organizing that information. Current business and organizational theory utilizes a system called a Mind Map.

This is where you take those random bits of data and place them in a sequential board. I use poster board but you can purchase and download some pretty elaborate mind mapping systems. The idea is to get it in a format that you can visually scrutinize.

This allows you to see a full picture of the possibility of all that can be included in the book. Your mind map takes the data dump a step further in that it begins to segment or place stuff everywhere.

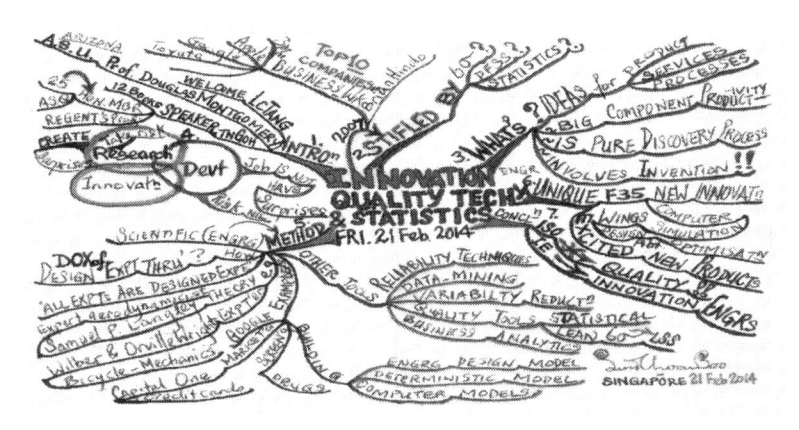

As you can see a plethora of possibility is presented. This leads to the next step which is called clumping.

Recap The Mind Map~

- ✓Mind mapping is gathering all your thoughts
- ✓Mind Mapping Considers Everything

- ✓ Just because you write you don't have to use
- ✓ Mind Maps give you a picture of everything
- ✓ Nothing is taboo on your Mind Map
- ✓ Getting it all out Helps
- ✓ It may feel stupid on the inside, but be brilliant
- ✓ A Mind Map shares every conceivable thought

## Step 6~Clump It

Clumping takes this disjointed thinking and begins to lump it together so it begins to form a pattern. This pattern is further enhanced by the connection that one or more of these parts may hold to one another.

Even then there is no guarantee or requirement that the clumped items be a part of this book. Everything stands on its own and is only as important as it relates to the finished product.

The purpose of Clumping is to Discover if there is a real need for the unloaded ideas or if they are unnecessary for this particular project. It may be that you have some really great ideas that will be included in future books.

A writer is always considering his next project. With the new technology a book may have a shelf life of a month maybe a year. There are so many new books being published every day it's no wonder that some authors are cranking out a book a month. With the new technologies it's possible to do that and more.

The clumping lets you tie together all connected parts and makes them a whole. When you do your Unload and the mind map, there tends to be a lot of overlap. You need to connect those dots and figure out what works with other stuff.

It may be that you have a complete chapter already mapped out for you and you can see that by looking at the connectedness of the Mind Map with the Clumping done. Most internet Mind Map programs have a feature that allows you to not only clump the pertinent items together but also to categorize them and reorganize them so you see the interconnectedness.

This technique alone will save you hours of frustration. You get to see what you have in place and also what you don't want in that sequence.

# Self Publish Your Own Book

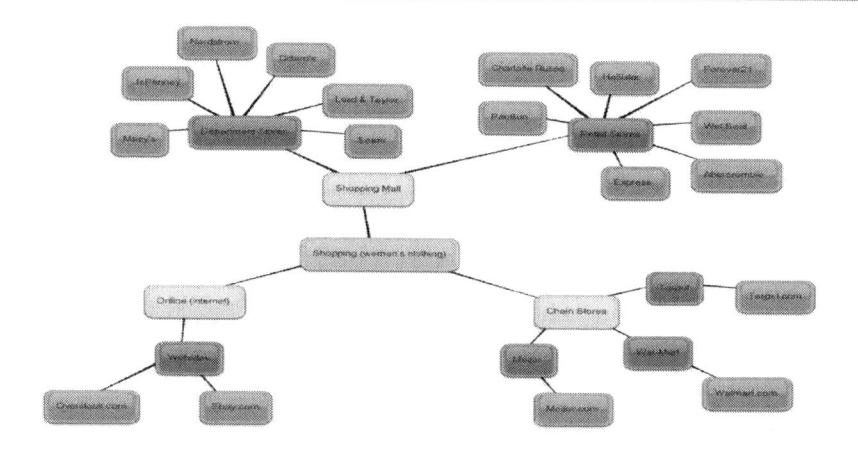

It's like a shopping mall, you can look in every store but you may only want to shop at Target. The Mind Map gives you a visual and the Clumping gives you a specific. If your desire is to go to Target you need to have a directory or map to chart a course to take you there.

The Mind map does it and shows you other places along the way. Clumping shows you all the stores that are similar and helps you decide which ones to shop at and which ones to avoid. If you are looking for shoes you would not go to jewelry store etc.

So Clumping is the action that takes all that disjointed information and joins it together so you can decide what to include and what not to include. Often there is so much you could include but in reality it just may be redundant and unnecessary.

Clump all you intended content and Then decide what yo finally include This will alleviate many headaches and double thoughts.

There can be a ton of possible content that you could include. Mind Mapping displays it all. The Clumping Procedure is a simple way to decide what goes where and what is not needed.

Recap: Clumping~
- ✓ Clumping Sorts relevant material
- ✓ Clumping organizes info into definable segments

- ✓ Clumping weeds out duplications
- ✓ Clumping highlights Necessary additions
- ✓ Clumping Exposes marginal material
- ✓ Clumping Determines what is in and What is out
- ✓ Clumping Discovers any missing pieces
- ✓ Clumping Sets up the Final outline
- ✓ Clumping Analyses and fixes Discrepancies

# Self Publish Your Own Book

## Step7~ Content

Once you have the initial aspects down and have a workable outline with included points and features, it is time to create the content. There are many ways to do this. In retrospect this may be the most troublesome part of the book creation process. you see this is the nuts and bolts of the book.

This is where you actually write it. There is no magic formula where you wish it and it happens. You could hire a ghostwriter and many people do. But for the regular run of the mill folks who want to write their own books there are some techniques that will help.

The simplest way is to take your outline and set aside some time to speak your book into existence. What I mean by that is to get a recording device like a Smartphone or computer with recording software and record the book.

You do this by following the outline and dictating it as if you are actually reading it aloud. The outline is what keeps you on track. Start at the introduction and speak /record the document as if you are reading it.

Your thoughts should be able to spill out on the recording as if you are reading it. The book that is in your mind now is presented to the recording format and is soon able to be transcribed into the first draft manuscript.

It is suggested that you take a few hours of uninterrupted time to record your book. This is how people are able to write their book in a weekend. There are inexpensive transcription services like Fiverr.com that will transcribe it for about a dollar a page. In the grand scheme of things that is very Cheap.

You are able to get a tremendous amount of material Written within a very short periods of time. If you already know what you want to say and you follow your outline you can seriously write your book overnight.

There are other ways to complete your book as well. The tried and true method is just to sit down and enter it into your computer. If you use this method you must have a disciplined manner to accomplish it.

The reason people have unfinished manuscripts is they don't have a scheduled disciplined approach to creating the content. You have to take that same outline and set aside a specific amount of time daily to accomplish the content creation.

I recommend that you schedule 45-50- minute session at intervals during each day for a week. this is more than enough time to complete a 100

-150 page book. Use some type of timer and get in a quiet place and follow your outline.

The key to all content creation is the outline. With a well thought out outline all you have to do is fill in the blanks. This prevents writers block and assures you stay on course.

When the timer goes off you need to get up stretch, move about and step away for at least 5 minutes. If you decide to continue, reset the timer and begin another 45-50 minute segment.

It is best that you only do two in a row. Afterwards takes a much longer break and return with another formatted time frame. By taking a hour or more break it keeps your mind fresh and reduces the possibility of distraction and boredom.

**Speak It**
- Get completed outline
- Record your book as if you are reading it aloud

**Write It**
- Get completed Outline
- Scedule blocks of 45-50 minutes and type away

Recap of Content development:

- ✓ Get your Outline Completed and visible
- ✓ Decide how to create content
- ✓ If you plan on speaking it, Schedule the time
- ✓ Make sure you have a quiet Place
- ✓ Get the required recording apparatus

- ✓ Record using the outline and like you are reading it
- ✓ Once complete send MP3 file to transcription service
- ✓ If you are going to write it: Schedule 45 minute each
- ✓ Follow your Outline(Think like it's a table of contents)
- ✓ Take a break after each 45-50 minute segment

# Self Publish Your Own Book

## Step 8~ Proof & Edit

Congratulations you have the hard part done. Now it time to fine tune. Proofing and Editing are two separate things. To proofread is to make sure you included everything you planned. One of my earlier books had a complete section missing. It was crucial, in that is was part of a structured acronym explanation.

Months later when I was reading it I discovered my mistake. Proofing prevents that from occurring. Proofing also repairs obvious errors and formatting mistakes. A good proofreader can save you a lot of headache. You are your own first proofer. A smart author always has a pair of extra eyes. You can be cheap and end up with a cheap work. Pay a little to get a lot.

Once you have had your manuscript proof read now it's time to edit. editing is where you add or delete content in order to convey the intended idea. All too often you may have something that is cute but in no way expresses what you intended.

Other times there may be spelling or grammatical errors that detract from the content and diminishes your credibility as a serious author.

Remember in today's marketplace, anyone can write a book. Yours has to have the added distinction of being good.

The discovered problem with the new Print On Demand (POD) technology is that everyone can publish a book. In the "old Days" Most books were weeded out by agents and publishers. They had the power to accept or reject a book. Their standards were high and they kept a very high profile of who got to be published and who didn't.

Subsequently many would be authors were locked out of the game. The only alternative were expensive vanity presses. They accepted anyone that was willing to pay.

Today's climate is unique and different. With print on Demand anyone can write and publish a book. There are no longer standards that keep out bad or badly written works. The new technology allows you to have an idea and follow through on it and have a published work.

Therefore (When you see "Therefore" you should find out what it is there for) it is incumbent on each author to adhere to higher and more lofty standards of quality and professionalism.

This new self policing will assure that books are still written and published with a personal code of responsibility and quality not just quantity. The editing and proofing process is where that begins. It is understandable that you want to keep your costs down to a minimum, but this is not the area to do so.

Please bear in mind there are unscrupulous agents out there ready to pounce on anyone desperate enough to want their book published. They will charge huge sums for poor or no quality work.

 Be sure that you vette out anyone that you use for any of your publishing services.  Just because someone has published a book doesn't mean that they know what they are doing.

The editing and proofing piece of your book will determine if you have a good book or a Great book.  Little things like obvious spelling errors or glaring grammatical errors can sink a book.

When it gets beyond just family and friends, the general public may not be so forgiving about those concerns. One bad review will torpedo ten good ones. Make sure your book has the advantage of several eyeballs and that at least one of them is a professional editor or reviewer.

The first book I wrote was reviewed by a professional at a major publishing firm. The report was that I had written what amounted to 3 books and that I should separate them and expand. I was vehement in my decision to keep the context of my content.

I published it ANYWAY and it languished in virtual cyberspace for a long time. I revisited it a while back and saw that indeed there was material for 3 or more books. I repacked it and released it and got critical review. I also discovered that I had left out an entire segment.

Bottom line...Get an Editor and Proofreader. They will save you time and will be well worth the investment.

Remember your book is a business venture. Just like any business venture it will require investment. I know that some of you are on a very tight budget. The only thing you gain by being cheap is a cheap product.

Determine what your budget will be up front and seek out services t hat fix in that budget. It is possible to write a book on a budget. But if you don't have to don't. Make the necessary investment to make it a great book.

Typically you can expect to invest at least $1000 in the production of your book. Costs include Proofing, Editing, Formatting, Cover Creation, Content and creation expenses, etc.

It is possible to cut those costs significantly by collaborating and learning how to do a lot of the items yourself. You can cut those costs down to next to nothing but never skimp on editing or proofreading.

Recap:

- ✓ Have your Book Proofed
- ✓ Have your book edited
- ✓ If you self Publish do not self Proof or Edit
- ✓ Order your printed proofs and let five friends read
- ✓ You might miss obvious points
- ✓ Look into services like Fiverr
- ✓ Editing and Proofing may cost but are worth it
- ✓ Don't skimp here
- ✓ Even on a budget you can get editing done

**Editing Plan**

_____

_____

_____

_____

Self Publish Your Own Book

## Proofing Plan

## Step 9~ Final Proof Yourself

When you have done with you editing and Proofing process, it is best if you re-read the book and do a final edit or proofing. Normally you will find one or two simple errors. the point is to be as thorough as possible with this stage. Back in publishing antiquity the high rate of rejection was due to poorly proofed works.

Now Content has something to do with that rejection too, but by and large the publisher received such poor quality and highly error prone Manuscript they just routinely tossed aside. The end result of doing a final once over is a better edited and formatted book that the public can appreciate.

# Self Publish Your Own Book

## Step10~CreateSpace

Now we come to the meat of the matter. Once your book has been written and proofed and edited it is time to publish it. There are a litany of POD (Print On Demand) publishers out there. I have had bad experiences and I have had Great Results. In My personal search for the perfect publisher I ran across CreateSpace.

I was looking for several things in a Publisher. I wanted one that produced professional looking books and did so a t a minimum cost and was easy to utilize. I was introduced to CreateSpace and have been a Fan every since. First off they are owned by Amazon. Amazon just happens to be the Largest bookseller on the planet. (Clue).

In addition they have over 500,000,000 million credit cards on file. They gives your book a fighting chance even for someone to stumble up on. More importantly they have developed a three folds cord that is not easily severed. You see they own Kindle and Audible as well.

This allows you to publish a printed book as well as an e-book(e-books have eclipsed Print sales and do so routinely). With the addition of Audible they also let you publish it as an audio book. This gets all three medium and increases your chance for exposure and success.

CreateSpace is an easy to use platform that offers an array of tools and support. Using their templates and easy to maneuver publishing tools you can be a published author overnight. They have taken the guest work out of the publishing process. They even provide free copy right and ISBN. This is huge in that you had to pay handsomely for those services in the past. Something as simple as an ISBN could delay your book for days if not weeks. They assign you one at no cost.

I will not get into great detail about your ISBN number, just suffice it to say your book needs one. It is how your book is identified and how the publishing company is designated. Unless you are planning on being a significant publisher on record, the ISBN Number that they assign you is more than sufficient. The Copyright procedure is done for you as well. The important thing is YOU maintain all the rights and privileges to your book and you were able to get them with huge royalties and little to no cost to you.

So let's dive right in to the process of publishing utilizing the CreateSpace Format. The VERY first thing you have to do is create a CreateSpace account. It is relatively simple but must be followed to the tee. You see certain information is important to be able to pay royalties and identify you as the owner of the rights and privileges to the book.

You are required to enter personal information like name and address. It also requires you to enter Social security info and banking data. This allows them to report your earnings and also identify you to the IRS. Even a small earnings must be reported as income. The advantage of the info being processed is that now you have a record to reduce your tax expenditures. Many people are reluctant to share this specific information in the setup process. You will not be able to proceed unless you provide Social Security Number and Banking information., This makes you a legitimate author. So get past it and provide it

Once you have a user name and Password you are ready to begin the journey. The very first thing you need to do is designate a title. This step is fluid. As we stated early on a title is important. But the good thing about the title is it can change as the book gets closer to completion. For the purpose of the publication process after getting your CreateSpace presence, the title is your first step. The steps to publication involve that as the starting point.

Fill in what you think you want the title to be you can always change that part later. Once you have selected a title you begin the 8 step process of creating you book for publication on CreateSpace. The next step is to indicate whether or not there is a subtitle. Subtitles are good to finish the thought invoked by the title. If you have a quirky title or one that is a bit ambiguous, the subtitle will help to clarify it. A good subtitle can make a GREAT title.

Once you have settled on the title and subtitle you need to share who the author and contributing authors are. If you are the only person being credited with the publication just state that and move on. If you are in collaboration with another or other writers you are able to indicate that as well. With the POD format more and more people are joining together and writing a book. The first book I wrote was a group of likeminded individuals writing together. You are also able to share contributing authors and the person writing the foreword. In any event this is the area to give credit to all connected with the project.

It should be noted that any professional names can be included here i.e. Dr. Rev. etc. It is best to not include such annotation if they are not earned or recognized. In the process of collecting this data the software will automatically upload it on the book to be displayed as such.

At this juncture you will need to select if this is a part of a series of just a single line book. You will also need to decide the language you will be printing in and the publication date. This is important because you may be planning a pre-launch and need to have the projected date of delivery.

As you progress through the info collection stage, next we need to make a choice as to which ISBN you will utilize. CreateSpace offers one at no cost and they are listed as the publisher on record. This is no big deal unless you plan on being an established publisher. If so, you will need to contact the agency called Bowder. They are the authorized entity in the US that markets ISBN numbers. You can purchase a single one for about $40 and blocks for a few hundred.

You can only use an ISBN once, so if you buy your own you have to be careful every time you change the book you have to use another ISBN. That could get costly. Until you are well established as an Author and publisher you might want to use the Free ones that CreateSpace provides.

This is the beginning of your cost cutting. You are required to select the free or personal number in order to proceed.

Once you have selected your number choice you will be directed to the size of your book. The standard size being used today is 6X9. This looks good and is easy to handle and carry around for potential book sales. In this section you will also be asked if you want the matte finish for the cover or the gloss. the Matte is very good looking and seems to hold up better than he gloss.

In that same vein you will need to pick the paper type and select if you want color or black and white. There are two paper types; white and cream. According to the type of book you are creating that will determine the type of paper and color to choose. Those choices' will also contribute to the final cost of the book as color is more expensive.

I know this seems like tedious work but relax you are almost done. You have now come to the juicy part...uploading the interior. It is best to format the Micro soft word file into a PDF file. This is the format of choice for CreateSpace although they recently went to an upload that allows you to go directly to upload form the Word doc. That sounds more complicated than it is.

 You just click on the browse button and select the file you want to upload. It may take a few minutes according to the size of the file. Once that upload is complete you will want to submit and save the work so done far. The system will begin initial determination as to whether the upload meets the style and format criteria. If it is formatted in such a way that the content is not in a specific area it may bleed out and make it difficult for the consumer to read. Pay attention to the perimeters and format directions here. This could save you hours on reformat and redo.

When your content has been preliminarily approved it is time to begin work on your cover design or upload. I cannot say enough about the cover. It is how people will decide to buy or not to buy. I know you may have heard "Don't Judge a book by its Cover" But that is precisely what people do. In this age when so many books are being written, in many cases all they have to go on is the cover.

I suggest you hire some one to do a professional cover. CreateSpace has 5 pages of really good cover templates. If you are techy and have some graphic design skills this may be something you can do for yourself. It is best to get a pro to do this though. A good cover from a company like 99 designs will cost about $99 and will be well worth it. I have had some great work done by Fiverr.com. They will produce a good cover for $5. Fiverr will get it to you in a matter of days and will do revisions until you are satisfied.

The CreateSpace Cover editor allows you to upload a predesigned cover or start from scratch using their cover creator. I like to use a Fiverr front and then follow up with using the cover creator to do the back cover. Either way is okay. The important thing is that you get a good cover done and submit it for review as well. While your SAVED cover and interior are being reviewed you are next directed to a description and BISAC coding

Your description is important for a number of reasons. It is what will be displayed on Amazon once the book is published. This gives you a chance to write a brief introduction to your book. When the 500,000,000 people are browsing on the Amazon website and just happen to see your beautiful book cover, they will want to know what it's all about. After all "You can't Judge a Book It's cover". This brief description will be the hook that gets people to take a chance on your book.

Take your time and make sure that your Description is complete and error free. this is the best chance you will have of getting new eyeballs to look at your book. A Great description will cause strangers to consider your book when you are an unknown.

The combination of a Great Cover and a strong Description will drive more traffic to your book than anything. Later we will discuss some traffic generation techniques. It will all be for naught if once they see the cover they are turned off and once they read the description they are not turned on.

This leads to the selection of the BISAC Code. This is a preselected categorizing tool that selects the niche you will be competing in. It is extremely important that you choose a correct and controllable category. If you select something not germane to your book content you could lose out of tons of FREE promotion from Amazon. The drop down menus in this section allows you to hone down your book detail to an area that separates you and segments you to a position of success. For this book I choose Language Arts and Disciplines & Authorship. There will not be a lot of completion here, yet it is the specific arena I am operating in. Later you will see why it is so important to take the time to categorize properly.

In my initial books I did not realize that Amazon places such a high value on which specific niche you segment. I just ignored those sections and probably missed out on the recognition of being a Best Seller 5 years ago when the competition was a lot less. Pay attention to the details and you will be successful every time. The details are crucial. For this aspect the details are zeroing in to the specific categories that best express your focus. Your BISAC code will zone you in to a core area that you can compete in. The beauty is that you do not have to compete against every book written. You get to zero in and only compete against those book in your chosen category.

As we go down the road to publishing with CreateSpace, next is the biography. This again is of high value because it will up load to your Amazon author page. I would like to also point out that you will also have a CreateSpace store. this is where you should direct customer to purchase as they give you a larger royalty.

## Step 11~ Kindle

This Year e-books are expected to reach 10 billion in sales. This is the unsung success story of the internet. In the last 5 years e=books have scaled up from nowhere to increasing Billions in revenue. This increase has been fueled by low or no cost e-book readers.

It is now possible to read e-books on PC's Laptops and even Smart phones. This technology upgrade has fueled an alliance with e-book publishers that has skyrocketed sales.

Authors who are publishing e-books many times are opting not to even publish a print book.

Most Speakers, Coaches, Pastors and Entrepreneurs prefer to have the print book because it gives visible credibility to their platform

Once you have completed the CreateSpace upload you have the Option to publish on Kindle. You must have an Amazon account and register for the KDP as well. KDP means Kindle Direct Publishing. You have several options in the KDP platform. I recommend you Okay the Kindle Select option. It gives you some great incentives which we will discuss later.

In order to be fully registered with KDP and Amazon you must enter your banking information so they can pay you and your Tax ID or Social Security # so they the track the income.

Many of my clients have balked at this requirement. Just suffice it to know that the IRS wants their share of your soon to be great income. This is not up for discussion. You will not be able to proceed further unless you supply it.

If you allowed CreateSpace to upload and convert your manuscript you have very little left to do. There are some housekeeping items that must be completed.

- You have to type in your title and list the Author(s)
- They ask for your ISBN #

- There is a section for BISAC this segments your entry
- You are prompted for 5 Keywords. This helps you get found on Google and Amazon
- The Next prompt is crucial...You are required to select 2 categories. The trick is to pick unique areas that have limited competition in it. It should be germane to the subject matter. The correct category will give you a better shot at ranking Higher in Amazon.
- Rounding out the KDP platform is the need to select

which markets you want to publish in and Pricing.
- Pricing is something that you have to consider carefully. First off you have to decide if you want 35% or 70% royalty
- To get 70% you have to price it between $2.99 and $9.99

## Self Publish Your Own Book

## Step 12~ ABS (Automatic Best Seller)

The last step in the process is to make your book an Amazon Best seller

Amazon uses a static format that is updated every hour. I had written 7 books before I discovered how to read the ranking report. Each book is rated based on number of pre-sales, number of sales, number of reviews and placement in specific niches.

That is why it is so important to pick the best category to compete in. The competitive edge is generated by burrowing down in to sub categories. This allows you stand out in a deeper sub group and garner higher rankings. When I finally discovered how to read the ranking I was blown away. It only takes a small number of sales to reach the best seller status.

I have found that pre-sales will give even higher ranking quicker. Amazon ranks on several levels. they compare you to the total book platform, and then your specific niche platform. There is also a ranking of "Hot New Releases"

This is how you rank against other new books for sale on Amazon. You could conceivably outrank an accomplished and well known author if you position your book properly.

I suggest you take a screen shot of where you book ranks. You can find your book ranking at the bottom of your book offering page. It is lost among a bunch of other information about the book.

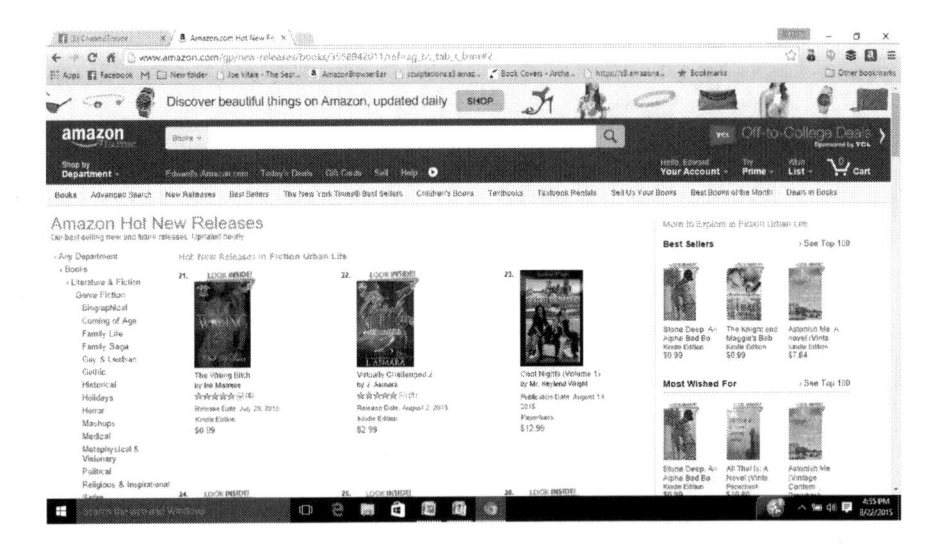

This is a screenshot of a recent best seller I published for Keylend Wright a new author who debuted in the top ten and eventually made it to number one.

# Self Publish Your Own Book

## Prologue:

I have given you a snapshot of what it takes to maneuver through the ever changing World of Self Publishing. It can be overwhelming. I suggest you get a coach for your first forays into the arena. Most people do not have editing or formatting skills.

I have seen publishing cost rage from $299 all the way up to $10,000. I am on a mission to bring fairness and focus to the field. If you want to have a decent book that is pleasing top look at and read you may need professional help. To invest $500 to $2000 to get a book that makes a strong statement about is not too much.

You have to study to keep abreast to the changing requirements and new envelopment of POD. It is my hope that this book serves as a guide to get you going and help you decide which direction to go in.